MT. ACONCAGUA
ARGENTINA / HEIGHT: 22,840 FEET / 6,962 METERS

MT. DENALI
(MCKINLEY) - UNITED STATES (ALASKA)
HEIGHT: 20,310 FEET / 6,190 METERS

AF068605

MT. ELBRUS
RUSSIA / HEIGHT: 18,510 FEET / 5,642 METERS

MT. EVEREST
NEPAL/TIBET
HEIGHT: 29,032 FEET / 8,849 METERS

MT. KILIMANJARO
TANZANIA / HEIGHT: 19,341 FEET / 5,895 METERS

THE SEVEN SUMMITS
These mountains represent the highest peaks on each of the seven continents. Climbing all seven is a major goal for mountaineers worldwide.

MT. KOSCIUSZKO
AUSTRALIA (MAINLAND)
HEIGHT: 7,310 FEET / 2,228 METERS

MT. VINSON
ANTARCTICA / HEIGHT: 16,050 FEET / 4,892 METERS

MOUNT KILIMANJARO

LEONARD BOGARAD

CREATIVE EDUCATION • CREATIVE PAPERBACKS

Published by Creative Education and Creative Paperbacks
P.O. Box 227, Mankato, Minnesota 56002
Creative Education and Creative Paperbacks
are imprints of The Creative Company
www.thecreativecompany.us

Design by Graham Morgan
Art direction by Blue Design (www.bluedes.com)

Images by Dreamstime/Extezy, cover, 1, Pecorb, 1; Getty Images/Andrew Castellano, 9, Anna Mardo, 38–39, Ayzenstayn, 2, 32, Buena Vista Images, 24, Chris Jackson, 22, Copyright Michael Mellinger, 36, David Du Plessis, 43, Hulton Deutsch, 18, Martin Harvey, 4–5, Massimo Mei, 10, Nan Zhong, 16; Unsplash/Crispin Jones, 31, 35, David Phan, 29, Hu Chen, 6; Wikimedia Commons/Alfred Shauri, 13, Ashley Pomeroy, 30, Christopher Michel, 25, Furado, 40, Johnmaxmena2, 44, Masa Sakano, 45, Michelle Maria, 41, Muhammad Mahdi Karim, 38, Noel Feans, 21, Rama, 20, RVBS, 26, Stig Nygaard, 17, Vakantie43, 14–15

Every effort has been made to contact copyright holders for material reproduced in this book. Any omissions will be rectified in subsequent printings if notice is given to the publisher.

Copyright © 2025 Creative Education, Creative Paperbacks
International copyright reserved in all countries.
No part of this book may be reproduced in any form
without written permission from the publisher.

Library of Congress Cataloging-in-Publication Data
Names: Bogarad, Leonard, author.
Title: Mount Kilimanjaro / Leonard Bogarad.
Other titles: Seven summits (Series)
Description: Mankato : Creative Education and Creative Paperbacks, 2025. | Series: Seven summits | Includes bibliographical references and index. | Audience: Ages 10–14 | Audience: Grades 4–6 | Summary: "Mount Kilimanjaro, a dormant volcano, is Africa's tallest peak and a Seven Summits mountaineering challenge. This guide for kids age 12 and up examines the mountain's geologic and climbing history. Includes a glossary, sidebars, profiles of notable climbers, and further resources"—Provided by publisher.
Identifiers: LCCN 2024030272 (print) | LCCN 2024030273 (ebook) | ISBN 9798889892731 (library binding) | ISBN 9781682776391 (paperback) | ISBN 9798889893844 (ebook)
Subjects: LCSH: Mountaineering—Tanzania—Kilimanjaro, Mount—Juvenile literature. | Kilimanjaro, Mount (Tanzania)—Juvenile literature.
Classification: LCC GV199.44.T342 B64 2025 (print) | LCC GV199.44.T342 (ebook) | DDC 796.5220967826—dc23/eng/20240701
LC record available at https://lccn.loc.gov/2024030272
LC ebook record available at https://lccn.loc.gov/2024030273

Printed in the United States of America

Glacier near the summit of Mount Kilimanjaro

CONTENTS

Introduction 8

Chapter 1: Lay of the Land 11

Chapter 2: Tanzanian Culture 19

Chapter 3: Plan and Prepare 27

Chapter 4: Climbing Kilimanjaro 37

Stories of the Summit 44

Glossary 46

Selected Bibliography 47

Websites 47

Index 48

MOUNT KILIMANJARO

INTRODUCTION

It's a challenge like no other, a test of physical and mental strength. The idea of conquering the tallest mountain on each of Earth's seven continents was first proposed by American explorer William Hackett in the 1950s. Hackett, himself, managed to scale five of the seven peaks. However, it was not until 1985 that Richard Bass became the first person to achieve this remarkable feat. He was joined by Frank Wells, who, sadly, lost his life in a helicopter crash before he could summit Mount Everest.

The quest to ascend the **Seven Summits** is a test of a climber's whole being. It demands technical skills, strategic planning, and financial resources. Each mountain offers its own set of dangers, such as **altitude sickness**, extreme and rapidly changing weather, avalanches, **crevasses**, and falling rocks and ice. Despite these difficulties, many climbers are driven by the excitement of adventure, personal growth, and the grand sense of accomplishment that comes with standing atop the world's tallest peaks. While Africa's Mount Kilimanjaro may not be the tallest or the most challenging climb, it holds a special place in the hearts of those who attempt its peak.

Peeking through the clouds, Mount Kilimanjaro towers above a campsite for climbers.

Earth's largest land animals, African elephants, live in the shadow of the world's tallest free-standing mountain.

CHAPTER 1: LAY OF THE LAND

The snow-capped giant called Mount Kilimanjaro rises above the plains of northeastern Tanzania, in Africa. This mountain is actually an inactive, or dormant, volcano with three volcanic cones, namely Kibo, Mawenzi, and Shira. The tallest among them is Kibo. Its peak, known as Uhuru ("freedom" in the Swahili language), stands at an altitude of 19,341 feet (5,895 meters) above sea level—the equivalent of more than 13 Empire State Buildings stacked one on top of the other! Kilimanjaro is not only the tallest mountain in Africa and one of the Seven Summits, but it is also the world's tallest free-standing mountain and one of the largest volcanoes on Earth.

Tanzania, the largest nation in East Africa, spans an area close to 1 million square miles (2.6 million square kilometers). That's roughly the size of the state of New York—times seven! About 40 percent of Tanzania's land is dedicated

MOUNT KILIMANJARO

to wildlife-protected areas, such as national parks, demonstrating the country's commitment to conservation of the natural world.

In addition to Mount Kilimanjaro's height, Tanzania is, indeed, a country of extremes. It is home to the Selous, Africa's largest game reserve, and the Serengeti, renowned for the Great Migration, which boasts the world's highest concentration of migratory animals. The country is bordered by Lake Victoria, the largest lake on the continent and a source of the Nile River, and Lake Tanganyika, the world's longest freshwater lake. These lakes were formed around 25 million years ago when the Great Rift Valley, which cuts straight through Tanzania and extends all the way into Asia, opened up due to **tectonic plate** activity.

The Earth's crust is comprised of seven major and several minor tectonic plates that move just under the planet's surface. These plates are tremendously huge underground rocks upon which the world's surface rests. Some are more than 60 miles (97 km) thick. When these plates collide, they buckle and form large mountain ranges. The Himalayas, for example, were formed by the collision of the Indian and Eurasian Plates about 50 million years ago. Sometimes, the plates disintegrate, due to immense internal forces, resulting in the creation of large valleys or rifts. The Great Rift Valley, where Mount Kilimanjaro is located, is an excellent example of a rift formed by the disintegration of a tectonic plate. This process also led to the formation of volcanoes along the Rift Valley. Kibo, the tallest of Kilimanjaro's

TALLEST AND OLDEST

Mount Kilimanjaro boasts the tallest trees in Africa. Reaching an impressive height of 270 feet (82 m), these giant trees belong to the mahogany family and are found in the mountain's cloud forest. They hold the distinction of being not only the tallest but also among the oldest trees on the continent, with an estimated age of 500 to 600 years old. Farther up the mountain, orange **lichens** grow at a rate of merely 0.02 inch (0.5 millimeter) per year—roughly the width of a grain of rice. Given their incredibly slow growth rate and how large some of them are, the lichens on Kilimanjaro could be thousands of years old, making them some of the planet's oldest living things.

CHAPTER 1: LAY OF THE LAND

MOUNT KILIMANJARO

Climbers encounter an ice field on Kilimanjaro's summit.

volcanic cones, has magma just 1,300 feet (396 m) below the surface. Some scientists speculate that it could erupt at any moment.

Kilimanjaro's mountain slopes feature five climate zones, each with its own unique vegetation and wildlife. At the base lies the cultivation zone. Its altitude ranges from 2,600 to 6,000 feet (792–1,829 m). This zone is characterized by village-centered undertakings, including farming and caring for livestock. The consistent rainfall and rich volcanic soil on the southern slopes of Kilimanjaro make it ideal for agriculture.

The next climate zone is the montane forest zone. Its altitude ranges from 6,000 to 9,200 feet (1,829–2,804 m). Wrapping around the entire mountain, this moist, humid region is a thriving tropical cloud forest. Like its name suggests, clouds and mist occur regularly there. The forest is filled with mosses and flowering plants such

MOUNT KILIMANJARO

as the stunning red hot poker. It serves as a habitat for blue monkeys and various colobus monkeys, along with a wide range of other animal species. Additionally, it is a haven for a multitude of bird species, including malachite sunbirds and crowned eagles.

From 9,200 to 11,000 feet (2,804–3,353 m) lies the heather and moorland zone. The dense trees of the montane forest zone seem to halt suddenly, revealing breathtaking views of Kilimanjaro's peaks. This area, adorned with

Kilimanjaro's heather and moorland zone

Vegetation thins along Kilimanjaro's hiking trails as the elevation increases.

shrubs and flowering plants called heathers, bears a striking resemblance to the Scottish Highlands, home of the mythical Loch Ness Monster.

Kilimanjaro's next climate zone is the highland alpine desert zone, ranging from 11,000 to 15,000 feet (3,353–4,572 m). Because of sparse rainfall, this zone is considered a desert. Only lichens grow there.

Everything above 15,000 feet (4,572 m) is part of the arctic summit zone. It includes the upper reaches of Kibo and consists of high altitude arctic conditions, which are challenging, inhospitable, and home to tremendous glaciers. This zone has only half the oxygen that is normally present at sea level.

Despite its abundant natural beauty, Mount Kilimanjaro's home country of Tanzania grapples with significant environmental challenges. Desertification is one of them. In this process, good farming soil turns to dry desert. Natural occurences, such as drought, may trigger it. So may human activities, such as poor agricultural practices and **deforestation**. Tanzania has one of the highest deforestation rates in Africa. Driving this practice is the need for more farmland. Negative effects of deforestation include habitat loss and the subsequent possibility of extinction for countless species, many of which may live only in those forests. Removing trees also removes their ability to help clean the air of carbon, increasing levels of greenhouse gases and contributing to climate change.

CHAPTER 1: LAY OF THE LAND

A Chagga chief in ceremonial dress, circa 1955

CHAPTER 2: TANZANIAN CULTURE

While the local economy greatly benefits from tourism, the **cultural** and spiritual value of Kilimanjaro to the Chagga, the people who reside upon its slopes, is of the utmost importance. Known to them as Kili, the mountain is a sacred place.

Tanzanians live by the national motto "Freedom and Unity," demonstrated by the peaceful coexistence of Christians and Muslims, unlike in many other parts of the world. If visitors show respect for Tanzanian customs and culture, they will be warmly welcomed. Tanzanian society is known for its kindness and courtesy. Proper introductions are greatly respected. If a visitor needs directions from someone on the street, it's considered polite to ask for permission to ask a question before actually asking it. A cheerful response is likely, often opening the door to conversation and perhaps even a friendship. One key tip for all visitors: It's essential to always ask for permission before taking a photograph

MOUNT KILIMANJARO

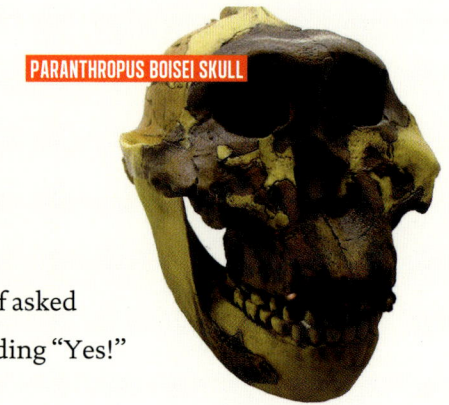

PARANTHROPUS BOISEI SKULL

of a Tanzanian. This is a significant point of manners. If asked courteously, locals will usually respond with a resounding "Yes!"

The Chagga, belonging to the Bantu **ethnic** group, hail from the Kilimanjaro region of Tanzania and represent the country's third most populous ethnic group. Historically, the Chagga resided in independent states on the slopes of Mount Kilimanjaro, where the essence of their culture is still embodied in village life. Largely agricultural, each village typically has one small store located in the center and a farmer's market. The villagers, who adhere mostly to traditional Chagga beliefs, often wear brightly colored clothing.

The faith system of the Chagga revolves around Mount Kilimanjaro. They believe their primary god, Ghost, resides on the summit. Before Christianity and Islam were introduced, the Chagga followed a religion that focused on nature and ancestor worship, a practice that continues to this day. They still make animal sacrifices to Ghost. Certain areas of the high forest are home to ancient shrines adorned with plantings of masale, a plant deemed holy. Kifunika Hill, a dormant volcano on the Marangu route, is also holy to the Chagga people. Visitors can easily sense that it is a deeply spiritual place.

In Tanzanian culture, professionals such as business people, lawyers, and doctors, often support their extended family members. This practice of resource sharing is a crucial aspect of their lifestyle—giving back the assistance they

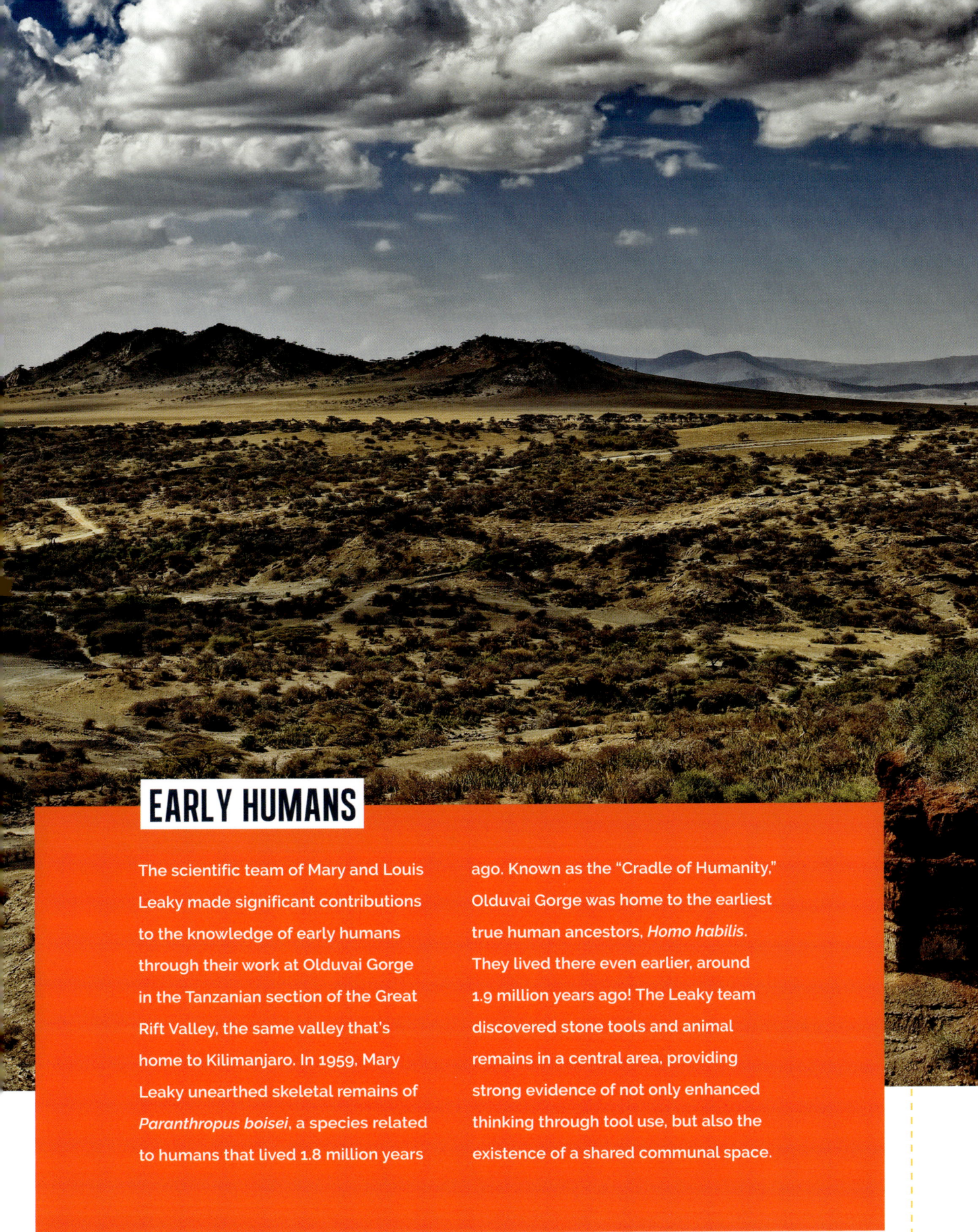

EARLY HUMANS

The scientific team of Mary and Louis Leaky made significant contributions to the knowledge of early humans through their work at Olduvai Gorge in the Tanzanian section of the Great Rift Valley, the same valley that's home to Kilimanjaro. In 1959, Mary Leaky unearthed skeletal remains of *Paranthropus boisei*, a species related to humans that lived 1.8 million years ago. Known as the "Cradle of Humanity," Olduvai Gorge was home to the earliest true human ancestors, *Homo habilis*. They lived there even earlier, around 1.9 million years ago! The Leaky team discovered stone tools and animal remains in a central area, providing strong evidence of not only enhanced thinking through tool use, but also the existence of a shared communal space.

HOW DO YOU SAY?

Swahili is the official language of two African nations: Tanzania and Kenya. It's also spoken frequently in neighboring Uganda and the Democratic Republic of the Congo. Although it's not necessary to speak Swahili to climb Mount Kilimanjaro, it is considered a courtesy to show a willingness to learn. Here are a few basic phrases:

Jambo (JAHM-boh) Hello

Tafadhali (tah-fah-DAH-lee) Please

Asante (ah-SAHN-tay) Thank you

Ndiyo (NEE-oh) Yes

Hapana (hah-PAH-nah) No

Samahani (sah-mah-HAH-nee) Sorry

Hakuna matata (hah-KOO-nah mah-TAH-tah) No problem, no worries

Pole, pole (POH-lay POH-lay) Slowly, slowly

Kwaheri (kwah-HAIR-ee) Goodbye

received from their parents. The Chagga community operates on principles of collective responsibility and mutual care.

Tanzania is home to at least 121 ethnic groups. More than 90 percent of Tanzanians speak Swahili. It is often possible to determine a person's region by their unique dialect, much like determining an American's home state. In Chagga culture, most issues are resolved collectively at the grass roots level. Individuals engage in discussions to reach solutions that are agreeable to the majority. They are accountable to everyone, fostering a sense of community-wide collaboration focused on the entire group's welfare.

The Chagga make up the most influential and economically successful groups in Tanzania. They attribute their prosperity to the fertile soil of Mount Kilimanjaro, their strong work ethic, and their effective farming practices. These practices include irrigation systems and ongoing organic fertilization methods, which have been used for thousands of years. Farmers also grow a variety of crops, including bananas, beans, and corn. The Chagga are particularly renowned for their Arabica coffee beans, which are exported around the world.

While the Chagga communicate in a Bantu language, their language includes several dialects somewhat akin to Kamba, which is spoken in southeast Kenya. Chief Kivoi, a distinguished Kamba trader, once scaled Kilimanjaro's Uhuru Peak before organizing and leading his extensive caravans northward to Kamba. His precise birth date remains unknown, but he is thought to have lived from the 1780s to 1852. The first Europeans to reach Kilimanjaro's summit were Hans Meyer and Ludwig Purtscheller, in 1889. Swahili Mwini Amani, two local leaders, and a number of **porters** accompanied Meyer and Purtscheller.

The Maasai people believe Kilimanjaro is a sacred place.

The Maasai often wear red to symbolize the area's red volcanic soil and the blood of their cattle.

Furthermore, a Tanzanian named Yohana Lauwo was also a member of the team that reached the summit at Uhuru Peak.

The Maasai, often seen near Kilimanjaro, are a prominent people recognizable by their vibrant red robes and large spears. They originally came from the dry central regions of Tanzania and Kenya but have since spread across all of Tanzania. They are peaceful, migratory people who travel, based on weather conditions, to areas suitable for their cattle to graze.

According to legend, Bantu Pygmies once lived on Kilimanjaro, as well, journeying across the mountain from east to west before settling in the Congo Basin. A unique story, found only in the Uru dialect common on Kilimanjaro, tells of other Pygmies who embarked on a journey in the reverse direction, from west to east, in search of timber for King Solomon.

CHAPTER 3: PLAN AND PREPARE

Advanced mountaineering skills aren't necessary to climb Mount Kilimanjaro. It's a "walk-up" journey. However, about half the climbers who attempt Kili don't reach the summit. Why? Because they haven't adequately planned and prepared.

Kilimanjaro doesn't require climbers to be world-class athletes, but they should be reasonably fit. That means starting training well before landing in Tanzania. The first step after booking with a licensed tour operator is to invest in an excellent pair of hiking boots. They don't need to be heavy-duty mountaineering boots. Sturdy, ankle-high boots that are waterproof and breathable will do. Buying them a size larger than usual is a smart idea so they can accommodate a thick pair of wool socks, as well as an insulating silk pair. Boots are the most crucial piece of gear for a Kili climber, so it's a good idea to shop around and try different styles.

MOUNT KILIMANJARO

A day backpack is the next item to get. It should have plenty of external pockets for easy access to rain gear, snacks, or equipment such as foldable, lightweight, carbon-fiber hiking sticks. With boots and backpack in hand, it's time to start training.

ost climbers will benefit from a steady exercise routine that incorporates weight training, core strengthening, and leg workouts. Wearing boots and carrying a loaded backpack while hiking hills or flights of stairs or using a Stairmaster at the local gym can help build endurance. A load of 20 to 25 pounds (9–11 kilograms) is a good place to start. Hiking at least 50 miles (80 km), in boots, with a loaded backpack and trekking poles, before setting off for Tanzania should be a goal. Training, particularly downhill walking, can reduce the likelihood of developing blisters while on the mountain.

When packing clothes for a Kilimanjaro adventure, layers are key. Temperatures may range from around 80 degrees Fahrenheit (27 degrees Celsius) in the town of Moshi, where most climbers find lodging, to as low as -20 °F (-29 °C) at Uhuru Peak. At lower elevations, it's advisable to wear lightweight hiking pants and lightweight long sleeves, despite the heat, as this can help avoid Anopheles mosquitoes, which carry malaria. Up the mountain, above the tree line, cold weather will be significant, so climbers should ensure that inner layers, including thermal underwear, are made of moisture-wicking synthetic fabric, not cotton or wool. A couple pairs of gloves will be

ALTITUDE SICKNESS

Acute Mountain Sickness (AMS), or simply "altitude sickness," strikes climbers at high elevations, usually triggering at about 10,000 feet (3,048 m). It's a common occurrence that happens to skilled and new hikers alike. Although usually not severe, AMS symptoms put added stress on a climber's body and may even keep a climber from summiting. Headache, dizziness, tiredness, difficulty breathing, nausea, and general discomfort appear 12 to 24 hours after reaching high alitude. Symptoms usually lessen by the third day, once the body adjusts to the elevation. Staying hydrated can help ward off symptoms, as can special altitude medication.

MOUNT KILIMANJARO

needed—one light pair and one heavy pair for summit day. A down-filled jacket rated to below 0 °F (-18 °C), which weighs little more than 5 pounds (2.3 kg), is essential. So are rain pants and an outer rain jacket that fits over everything, including one's backpack. A wide-brimmed hat with a chin strap comes in handy on sunny, windy days, while a warm wool hat that covers the ears is perfect for summit day.

Given the altitude, and the thin atmosphere, the sun's UV rays are even more intense up on the mountain. Glacier sunglasses are specifically designed to protect climbers' eyes from sun damage. It's crucial to wear sunscreen and lip balm with an SPF of 50+ or higher and reapply it several times a day, even in cloudy weather. If using a mosquito repellent to help protect against malaria, it's recommended to apply a 30 percent **Deet** repellent to all exposed skin about 30 minutes after applying sunscreen to prevent the sunscreen from being washed off. All clothing and gear should be pretreated with the insecticide Permethrin. Caution should be used when applying it, however, as it is toxic when wet.

Tour operators usually supply porters to carry climbers' duffel bags up and down Kili. For the porters' safety, there's a weight limit of 44 pounds (20 kg) per bag, so climbers must weigh their bags prior to going to Africa. Duffle bags should be heavy-duty and include the climber's name permanently marked on the sides and bottom.

Trekking poles help climbers maintain balance and ease stress on leg joints by redistributing weight.

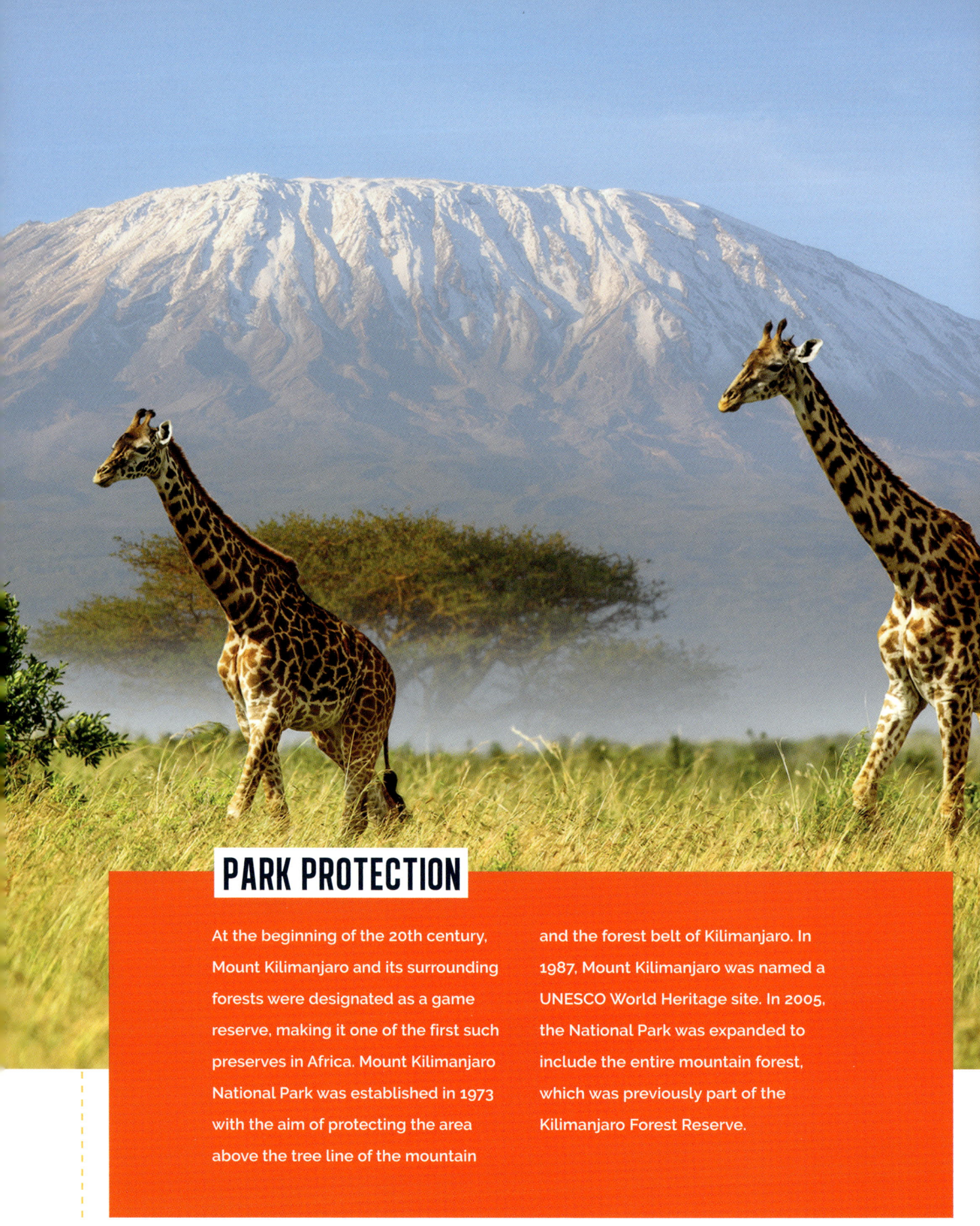

PARK PROTECTION

At the beginning of the 20th century, Mount Kilimanjaro and its surrounding forests were designated as a game reserve, making it one of the first such preserves in Africa. Mount Kilimanjaro National Park was established in 1973 with the aim of protecting the area above the tree line of the mountain and the forest belt of Kilimanjaro. In 1987, Mount Kilimanjaro was named a UNESCO World Heritage site. In 2005, the National Park was expanded to include the entire mountain forest, which was previously part of the Kilimanjaro Forest Reserve.

Most climbers pack the following basics: a first-aid kit, wipes, toilet paper, moleskin for potential blisters, ear plugs for sleeping, and ibuprofen, which not only provides pain relief but also can treat mild altitude sickness.

A water purification system is a must, unless the tour operator provides purified water. Most operators today do. All water consumed on the climb, including ice cubes, must be purified to kill any germs it may contain. Climbers are encouraged to drink at least 170 ounces (5 liters) of water per day. Guides often say "Sippy, sippy" to remind climbers to drink. An insufficient amount of water will cause headaches and potentially prevent a climber from reaching the summit due to altitude sickness.

Additional items to pack include Nalgene water bottles with insulators to prevent them from freezing solid. A headlamp is required for night reading in camp and going to the bathroom in the dark. It's most important on summit day, which typically starts around midnight, as climbers ascend Kili in the pitch black of night until sunrise at around 4:00 or 5:00 a.m. A spare headlamp, extra batteries, a solar-powered charger, trekking poles, a journal, and a pen for recording experiences are all worth bringing. And the final essential piece of gear is a waterproof sleeping bag, which should be down-filled and rated for below 0 °F (-18 °C). A sleeping mat and an inflatable bed are also recommended. Tents are almost always provided by the tour operator.

In addition to clothing, gear, and equipment, travel insurance is a must-have. Good policies cover illnesses, accidents, medical travel back home, and cancellations up to altitudes of 19,700 feet (6,005 m). Another must-have is a credit/debit card and plenty of cash. The national currency is the Tanzanian

MOUNT KILIMANJARO

Shilling, which can be obtained at hotels or ATMs, but U.S. dollars are widely accepted, too.

Not every climber is the same, nor is every climbing experience on Mount Kilimanjaro. However, the following tips may help turn a good adventure into a great one:

- Create a packing list. That way, nothing critical is forgotten.

- Instead of packing hiking boots, wear them on the plane, in case luggage gets lost, and carry on any prescription medications, a cell phone, travel documents, wallet, cash, credit/debit card, valid passport, plane tickets, and vaccination certificates.

- Consult a doctor about malaria prevention and perhaps obtaining Diamox to prevent altitude sickness.

- Try on all gear and take any medications prior to leaving for Tanzania to avoid discovering an unexpected allergy.

- Eat well at every meal, even at high altitudes, where nausea may be a factor.

- Breathe deeply in the arctic zone, as the natural tendency there is to take quick, short breaths, due to reduced oxygen.

Climbing tour group size may vary from 2 to 20 hikers, depending on the company.

CHAPTER 4: CLIMBING KILIMANJARO

East Africa's long rainy season spans from March to early May, and its short rainy season occurs from November to the first half of December. Consequently, the best months for climbing Mount Kilimanjaro are late May through October. Another favorable period is from mid-December to late February. This later period would be an ideal time to pair a mountain climb with a safari, as Africa's Great Migration occurs during this timeframe.

Kilimanjaro welcomes more than 40,000 trekkers each year, partly because it's possible to walk to the summit without ropes or technical climbing experience. Although ice axes and crampons aren't needed, the climb is still challenging. It's also an expensive undertaking, so it's worth spending time to consider the best route to take to Uhuru Peak. An average climb takes five to nine days. The more time time spent on the mountain, the better a climber's body can acclimatize to the increasing altitude. On some days, early in the journey, hikers will pass through lush jungle accompanied by wildlife. On

MOUNT KILIMANJARO

others, especially on summit day, they will walk on loose rock, sliding back a half step for every step taken. Because of the changing conditions along the way, it's important to prepare mentally for the challenges ahead.

Mindfulness refers to being fully present in the moment, without thought, judgment, or interpretation. It's best to practice mindfulness before arriving at Kilimanjaro so it can easily be applied during a climb. Being mindful not only ensures that a climber doesn't miss the stunning beauty of the mountain and its surroundings, but it also keeps them focused on the present moment—from maintaining one's footing to not getting disheartened by the seemingly impossible distance still ahead. Mindfulness contributes to maintaining a positive mental attitude.

AFRICAN ELEPHANT

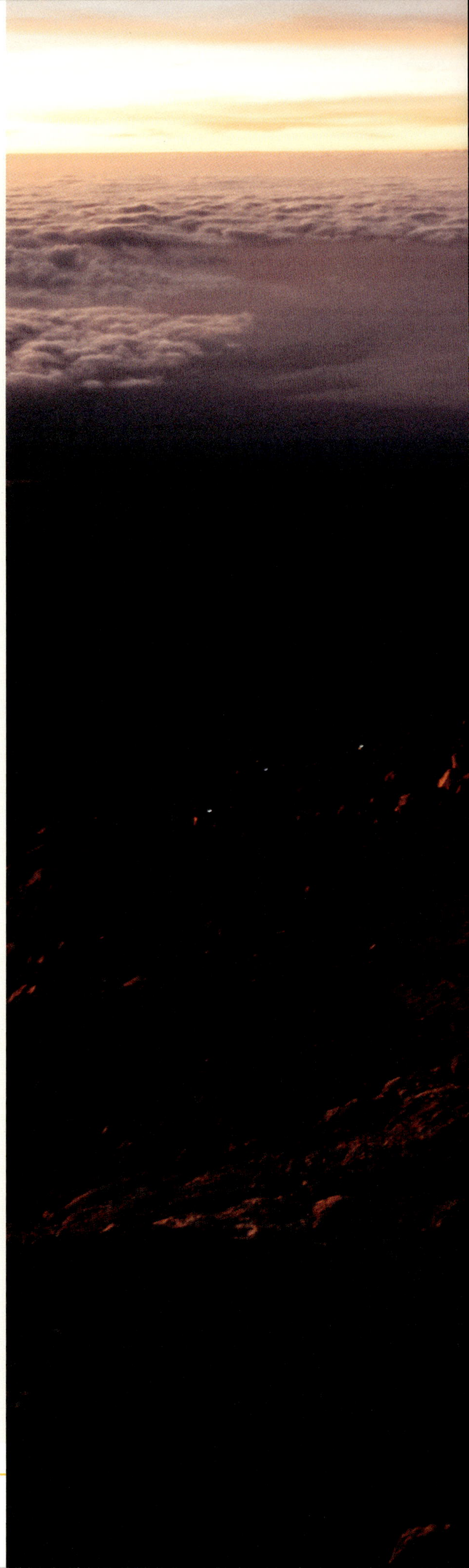

TIPPING

At the end of every Kilimanjaro journey is a tipping ceremony. Although guides, cooks, and porters receive a wage from the tour agency, it's customary to show appreciation for their care and assistance by tipping. Online and elsewhere, there are many opinions on what constitutes a fair tip, but, per day, climbers should expect to tip the senior guide $35, assistant guides $25, cooks $20, and porters $10. Tips should be handed, in envelopes, directly to each person, along with a warm thank-you.

MOUNT KILIMANJARO

Kili climbers are reminded to stay in communication with their climbing team at all times, especially their guide, and alert them to any difficulties. It's important to hydrate adequately, eat well, go slowly, and be prepared to descend if necessary before making the final push to Uhuru Peak. Of utmost importance is to leave no trace on Kilimanjaro. Pack out everything that's brought in.

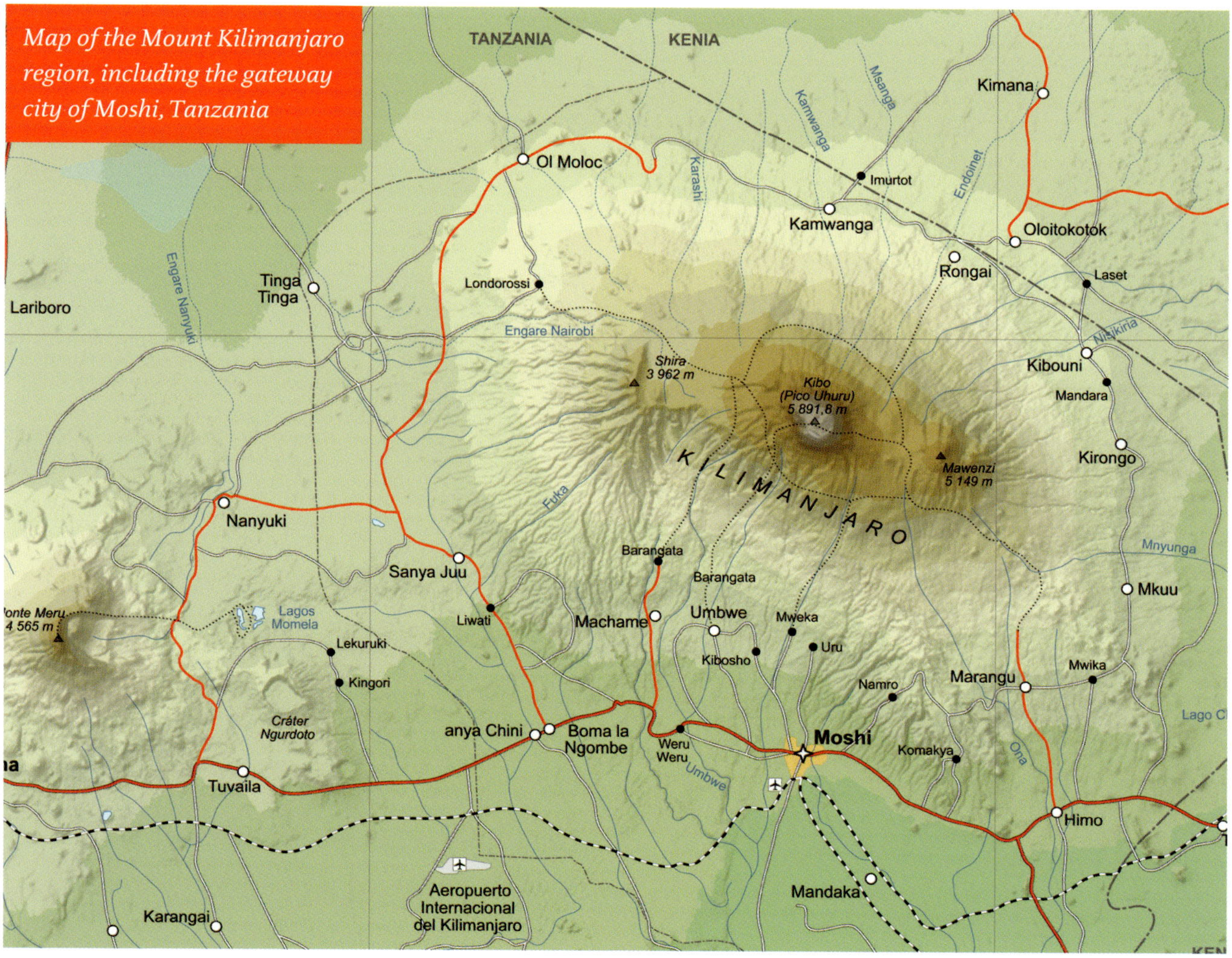

Map of the Mount Kilimanjaro region, including the gateway city of Moshi, Tanzania

Above-the-clouds aerial view of Mount Kili

The following are routes up Mount Kilimanjaro:

Machame Route (Whiskey Route)—This is the most popular route, due to its ascent via the southern slope, high success rate, and stunning landscapes. The 7-day route has an average summit success rate of more than 85 percent.

Marangu Route (Coca-Cola Route)—Recognized as the shortest route to the summit, it is easier to climb than the Machame route. However, it provides less acclimatization time, resulting in a much lower success rate. The route is not known for its scenery, but it is still the second most popular, due to its low level of difficulty and its huts equipped with beds and showers (all other routes offer tents). The success rate is just 27 percent for a 5-day route, 44 percent for a 6-day route, and 64 percent for a 7-day route.

Lemosho Route—Originating from the western side of the mountain, this route offers climbers plenty of acclimatization opportunities. Crowds are low, and there are spectacular scenic views. The 8-day option boasts a success rate of about 90 percent, while the 7-day route has around an 85 percent success rate.

Northern Circuit Route—This is the newest and longest route, taking 8 to 10 days. It initially follows the same path as the Shira plateau, one of the highest plateaus on Earth, before turning north and continuing around the backside of Kili to reach the summit via Gilman's Point. It offers excellent

MOUNT KILIMANJARO

acclimatization time and beautiful scenery, with an average summit success rate of up to 98 percent.

Rongai Route—Starting near the Kenyan border, this popular route ascends the northern side of the mountain. It offers a unique wilderness experience in the early stages of the climb. With beautiful views and fewer people, it offers a true hiking experience. The success rate is 85 percent for the 7-day option.

Shira Route—While scenic and less crowded, this route can pose acclimatization challenges, as it starts at 11,800 feet (3,597 m). An extra day is strongly recommended to get used to the high altitude. The success rate for the 6-day route is about 55 percent. For the 7-day route, the success rate is about 75 percent.

Umbwe Route—Previously classified as a technical mountaineering route, Umbwe has a particularly steep section leading to the summit and is recommended solely for experienced climbers with proper equipment. The success rate for the 5-day route is about 50 percent and 70 percent for the 7-day route.

When selecting a route up Kili, consider factors such as acclimatization to altitude, route complexity, the average number of other climbers on the route, and the beauty of the landscape. The Machame and Lemosho routes are often recommended as the best options on the southern side of Kilimanjaro. However, if time and resources aren't issues, the less traveled Northern Circuit route, with a success rate of more than 95 percent, is a strong alternative. Furthermore, talking to those who have successfully summited Mount Kilimanjaro, including guides, can be extremely valuable.

TO THE TOP

Several celebrities have summited Mount Kilimanjaro, including *Jurassic Park* author Michael Crichton and British actor Brian Blessed. In 2010, an MTV-sponsored trek brought actors Jessica Biel, Isabel Lucas, and Emile Hirsch, along with singers Kenna and Lupe Fiasco, to the summit. Mandy Moore successfully climbed Kili during a break from shooting the TV show *This Is Us* in 2018. Etuini Haloti Ngata, one of the greatest defensive linemen in the National Football League (NFL), announced his retirement in 2019 upon reaching Uhuru Peak, holding high a banner that read, "I'm retiring from the NFL on top."

CHAPTER 4: CLIMBING KILIMANJARO

MOUNT KILIMANJARO

STORIES OF THE SUMMIT

CHRISTOPHER HOWARD LONG

Born in California in 1985, Christopher Howard Long had an illustrious career in the NFL spanning 11 seasons, during which he played for the St. Louis Rams, the New England Patriots, and the Philadelphia Eagles. He won Super Bowl titles with both the Patriots and the Eagles. In 2013, Chris and former Seattle Seahawks player Nate Boyer embarked on a new project together: Conquering Kili. The program's mission is to provide clean water to communities in Africa and the United States. Combat veterans and NFL alumni are invited to summit Kilimanjaro's Uhuru Peak and, in the process, raise funds for the program.

Since launching Conquering Kili, Chris has successfully climbed Mount Kilimanjaro three times. Each climb symbolized the lengthy and grueling daily treks many African women undertake to fetch water for their families. Globally, more than 884 million people do not have access to safe drinking water. Conquering Kili has financed projects to construct wells, enhance water delivery systems, and much more. An outstanding achievement of the 2017 Conquering Kili summiting class was the funding of Well Site #20 in Sanya Station, situated in the Kilimanjaro region. This well, which produces about 2,641 gallons (9,997 L) of water per hour, services 7,500 Massai villagers. It has eliminated a 5-mile (8-km) journey to their previous water source, saving more than 1.6 million walking hours annually.

ERICK KIVELEGE

Erick Kivelege, a professional mountain climbing guide licensed by Tanzania National Parks, was born and raised in Moshi Town, Tanzania, in the shadow of Mount Kilimanjaro. Guiding people to the summit has been his life's mission. He has led thousands of people to the top and has reached the summit himself more than 500 times. Erick is also the author of the book *Climbing Kilimanjaro with Africa's Top Guide*.

Personable and proud of his homeland, Erick extends a warm welcome to everyone who wants to explore East Africa and Kilimanjaro. He is generous and open-hearted. "People in my family know that if they need something, I will share money when I have it," he says in his book. "This is common in Tanzanian life. When I return from a trip, people will say, 'Okay, you went up the mountain last week, and you came back down, so you have something.' That is how we do things here. We take care of others. This is Tanzania." He adds, "People in villages know how to enjoy life, family, and friends, and you might learn something from this and take it home with you.... You can almost hear the ancient drumbeats of our ancestors as you walk around [a village]; it is both comforting and deeply moving. It will feel like the land itself is alive with wonder, and that adventure is just around the next bend in the trail."

MOUNT KILIMANJARO

GLOSSARY

acclimatize—to adjust or get used to a new environment

altitude sickness—swelling of the lungs or brain caused by air pressure at high altitudes

crampon—a metal plate with spikes attached to a boot for walking or climbing on rock or ice

crevasse—a deep crack in a glacier or other body of ice

cultural—relating to a particular group in a society that shares behaviors and characteristics that are accepted as normal by that group

deforestation—purposely removing large areas of trees for timber or to clear land for farming, grazing, or construction

ethnic—of or relating to a large group of people connected by common racial, national, tribal, religious, linguistic, or cultural origin

lichen—an organism made up of fungus and algae growing in partnership

malaria—a life-threatening disease spread to humans through the bites of Anopheles mosquitoes infected with the parasite Plasmodium

porter—a person employed to carry luggage and other heavy loads

Seven Summits—a group that includes the tallest mountain on each of the seven continents

tectonic plate—a huge, rocky piece of Earth's shell that slowly moves around the world, carrying the continents and the ocean floor with it

SELECTED BIBLIOGRAPHY

Belanger, Jeff. T*he Call of Kilimanjaro: Finding Hope above the Clouds*. Watertown, Mass.: Charlesbridge Publishing, 2021.

Carmichael, Stephen, and Susan Stoddard. *Climbing Mount Kilimanjaro*. Bloomington, Ill.: Medi-Ed Press, 2002.

Fitzpatrick, Mary. *Tanzania*. Melbourne, Vic.; London: Lonely Planet, 2002.

Hamill, Mike. *Climbing the Seven Summits: A Comprehensive Guide to the Continents' Highest Peaks*. Seattle, Wash.: Mountaineers Books, 2012.

Stahl, Kathleen M. *History of the Chagga People of Kilimanjaro*. London: Mouton, 1964.

Treisman, Rachel. "Mount Kilimanjaro Climbers Can Share Slope Selfies in Real-Time Thanks to New Wi-Fi." NPR. August 22, 2022. https://www.wfae.org/2022-08-22/mount-kilimanjaro-climbers-can-share-slope-selfies-in-real-time-thanks-to-new-wi-fi.

Wexcomb, Catherine. "The Seven Summits According to Richard Bass." *Base Camp Magazine*. March 17, 2019. https://basecampmagazine.com/2019/03/17/seven-summits-according-richard-bass.

WEBSITES

7 Summits Club
https://7summitsclub.com
Learn about the world's tallest peaks and the people who climb them.

Kilimanjaro
https://www.britannica.com/place/Kilimanjaro
Discover facts about Africa's grand peak.

Kilimanjaro National Park
https://whc.unesco.org/en/list/403
Review facts, photos, and videos of this natural wonder.

MOUNT KILIMANJARO

INDEX

Aconcagua, Mount, 1
Acute Mountain Sickness (AMS), 8, 29, 33, 34
Amani, Mwini, 23
Bantu Pygmies, 25
Bass, Richard, 8
celebrity summiteers, 43
Chagga people, 18, 19, 20, 23
Chief Kivoi, 23
climate zones, 14, 16, 17
climbing
   equipment, 28, 31, 33, 42
   gear, 27, 28, 30, 31, 33, 34
   mindfulness, 38
   season, 37
   supplies, 28, 33 34
   tips, 34, 40
   training, 27, 28
Conquering Kili, 44
deforestation, 17
Denali (McKinley), Mount, 1
Elbrus, Mount, 1
Everest, Mount, 1, 8
glaciers, 6, 17
Great Rift Valley, 12, 21
Hackett, William, 8
Kilimanjaro, Mount
   first European summiteers, 23
   formation, 12
   height, 1, 11
   location, 1, 11, 12
   nickname, 19
   number of visitors, 37
Kivelege, Erick, 45
Kosciuszko, Mount, 1
Lauwo, Yohana, 25
Leaky, Mary and Louis, 21
Long, Christopher Howard, 44

malaria, 28, 30, 34
Maasai people, 24, 25, 44
Meyer, Hans, 23
Mount Kilimanjaro National Park, 32
Ngata, Etuini Haloti, 43
Olduvai Gorge, 21
porters, 23, 30, 39
Purtscheller, Ludwig, 23
routes
   Lemosho, 41, 42
   Machame (Whiskey), 41, 42
   Marangu (Coca-Cola), 20, 41
   Northern Circuit, 41–42
   Rongai, 42
   Shira, 42
   Umbwe, 42
Seven Summits, 1, 8, 11
Swahili language, 11, 22, 23
Tanzania, 8, 11–12, 17, 19, 20, 21, 23, 25, 27, 28, 34, 40, 45
tectonic plates, 12
temperatures, 28
tipping ceremonies, 39
vegetation, 14, 16, 17
Vinson, Mount, 1
volcanic cones, 11
   Kibo (Uhuru), 11, 12, 17, 23, 25, 28, 37, 40, 43, 44
   Mawenzi, 11
   Shira, 11
volcanoes, 11, 12, 20
Wells, Frank, 8
wildlife, 10, 12, 14, 16, 17, 37, 38